KEEPSAKES

SUMMER

To/
My very dear friend
Thinking of you always
January 1997.

CLB 4390
Published 1995 by CLB Publishing
Exclusively for Selectabook Ltd, Devizes
© 1995 CLB Publishing, Godalming, Surrey
ISBN 1-85833-291-5

Printed in Hong Kong by Imago

KEEPSAKES

SUMMER

Compiled by
Jean Thornhill

SELECT
EDITIONS

Eternal Summer

Shall I compare thee to a summer's day?
  Thou art more lovely and more temperate:
Rough winds do shake the darling buds of May,
  And summer's lease hath all too short a date:
Sometimes too hot the eye of heaven shines,
  And often is his gold complexion dimm'd:
And every fair from fair sometime declines,
  By chance, or nature's changing course, untrimm'd.
But thy eternal summer shall not fade
  Nor lose possession of that fair thou owest;
Nor shall Death brag thou wanderest in his shade,
  When in eternal lines to time thou growest:—
So long as men can breathe, or eyes can see,
  So long lives this, and this gives life to thee.

WILLIAM SHAKESPEARE

Sun and Shadow

THE UNIVERSAL STARE made the eyes ache. Towards the distant line of Italian coast, indeed, it was a little relieved by light clouds of mist, slowly rising from the evaporation of the sea, but it softened nowhere else. Far away the staring roads, deep in dust, stared from the hill-side, stared from the hollow, stared from the interminable plain. Far away the dusty vines overhanging wayside cottages, and the monotonous wayside avenues of parched trees without shade, drooped beneath the stare of earth and sky.... Everything that lived or grew, was oppressed by the glare; except the lizard, passing swiftly over rough stone walls, and the cicala, chirping his dry hot chirp, like a rattle. The very dust was scorched brown, and something quivered in the atmosphere as if the air itself were panting.

Blinds, shutters, curtains, awnings, were all closed and drawn to keep out the stare. Grant it but a chink or keyhole, and it shot in like a white-hot arrow. The churches were the freest from it. To come out of the twilight of pillars and arches – dreamily dotted with winking lamps, dreamily peopled with ugly old shadows piously dozing, spitting, and begging – was to plunge into a fiery river, and swim for life to the nearest strip of shade.

CHARLES DICKENS

Summer Morning

The meek-ey'd morn appears, mother of dews,
    At first faint-gleaming in the dappled east:
Till far o'er ether spreads the widening glow;
    And, from before the lustre of her face,
White break the clouds away. With quicken'd step,
    Brown night retires. Young day pours in apace,
And opens all the lawny prospect wide.
    The dripping rock, the mountain's misty top,
Swell on the sight, and brighten with the dawn.
    Blue, thro' the dusk, the smoking currents shine;
And from the bladed field the fearful hare
    Limps, awkward: while along the forest-glade
The wild-deer trip, and often turning gaze
    At early passenger. Music awakes,
The native voice of undissembled joy;
    And thick around the woodland hymns arise.
Rous'd by the cock, the soon-clad shepherd leaves
    His mossy cottage, where with Peace he dwells;
And from the crowded fold, in order, drives
    His flock, to taste the verdure of the morn.

JAMES THOMSON

Garden Duties

 ULY. TO BE DONE in the parterre and flower garden. Slip stocks and other lignous plants and flowers. From henceforth to Michaelmas you may also lay gilly-flowers and carnations for increase, leaving not above two or three spindles for flowers, with supports, cradles, and hooses, to establish them against winds, and destroy earwigs.

The layers will (in a month or six weeks) strike root, being planted in a light loamy earth mixed with excellent rotten soil and sifted. Plant six or eight in a pot to save room in winter. Keep them well from too much rains, but shade those which blow from the afternoon's sun, as in the former months.

Take up your early autumnal cyclamen, tulips and bulbs (if you will remove them, etc) before mentioned, transplanting them immediately, or a month after if you please, and then cutting off, and trimming the fibres, spread them to air in some dry place.

Gather now also your early cyclamen seeds, and sow it presently in pots. Likewise you may now take up some anemonies, ranunculus, crocus, crown imperial, Persian iris, fritillaria, and colchicums, but plant the three last as soon as you have taken them up, as you did the cyclamens.

DION CLAYTON CALTHROP

For Summer Time

Now the glories of the year
May be viewed at the best,
And the earth doth now appear
In her fairest garments drest:
    Sweetly smelling plants and flowers
    Do perfume the garden bowers;
Hill and valley, wood and field,
Mixed with pleasure profits yield.

Much is found where nothing was,
Herds on every mountain go,
In the meadows flowery grass
Makes both milk and honey flow;
    Now each orchard banquets giveth,
    Every hedge with fruit relieveth;
And on every shrub and tree
Useful fruits or berries be.

Other blessings, many more,
At this time enjoyed may be,
And in this my song therefore
Praise I give, O Lord! to Thee.

GEORGE WITHER

Hill View

JULY 4TH 1857 This morning opened still misty, but with a more hopeful promise than yesterday, and when I went out, after breakfast, there were gleams of sunshine here and there on the hillsides, falling, one did not exactly see how, through the volumes of cloud. Close beside the hotel of Inversnaid is the waterfall; all night, my room being on that side of the house, I had heard its voice, and now I ascended beside it to a point where it is crossed by a wooden bridge. There is thence a view, upward and downward, of the most striking descents of the river, as I believe they call it, though it is but a mountain-stream, which tumbles down an irregular and broken staircase in its headlong haste to reach the lake. It is very picturesque, however, with its ribbons of white foam over the precipitous steps, and its deep black pools, overhung by black rocks, which reverberate the rumble of the falling water. J. and I ascended a little distance along the cascade, and then turned aside; he going up the hill, and I taking a path along its side which gave me a view across the lake. I rather think this particular stretch of Loch Lomond, in front of Inversnaid, is the most beautiful lake and mountain view that I have ever seen.

NATHANIEL HAWTHORNE

Loch Lomond
E. Longstaffe

The Sweet o' the Year

Now the frog, all lean and weak,
   Yawning from his famished sleep,
Water in the ditch doth seek,
   Fast as he can stretch and leap:
     Marshy king-cups burning near
     Tell him 'tis the sweet o' the year.

Now the May-fly and the fish
   Play again from moon to night;
Every breeze begets a wish,
   Every motion means delight:
     Heaven high over heath and mere
     Crowns with blue the sweet o' the year.

Now all Nature is alive,
   Bird and beetle, man and mole;
Bee-like goes the human hive,
   Lark-like sings the soaring soul:
     Hearty faith and honest cheer
     Welcome in the sweet o' the year.

GEORGE MEREDITH

Garden Notes

 ULY 1789. My garden is in high beauty, abounding with solstitial flowers such as roses, corn-flags, late orange-lillies, pinks, scarlet lychnises, etc. The early honeysuckles were in their day full of blossoms, and so fragrant that they perfumed the street with their odour. The late yellow honeysuckle is still in high perfection and is a most lovely shrub; the only objection is that having a limber stem, and branches, it does not make a good standard.

July 5. My scarlet strawberries are good.... A peat-cutter brought me lately from Cranmoor a couple of snipe's eggs which are beautifully marbled. They are rather large, and long for the size of the bird, and not bigger at the one end than the other. The parent birds had not sat on them. These eggs, I find since, were the eggs of a Churn-owl. The eggs of snipes differ much from the former in size, shape and colour. The peat-cutter was led into the mistake by finding his eggs in a bog, or moor.

July 15. We have planted-out vast quantities of annuals, but none of them thrive. Grapes do not blow, nor make any progress. The wet season has continued just a month this day. Dismal weather!

GILBERT WHITE

Bringing in the Crops

Now go the mowers to their slashing toil,
   The meadows of their riches to despoil,
With weary strokes, they take all in their way,
   Bearing the burning heat of the long day.
The forks and rakes do follow them amain,
   Which makes the aged fields look young again.
The groaning carts do bear away this prize
   To stacks and barns where it for fodder lies.

With sickles now the bending reapers go
   The rustling tress of terra down to mow,
And bundles up in sheaves the weighty wheat,
   Which after manchet makes for kings to eat.
The barley, rye, and peas should first had place,
   Although their bread have not so white a face.
The carter leads all home with whistling voice,
   He plowed with pain, but reaping doth rejoice.
His sweat, his toil, his careful, wakeful nights,
   His fruitful crop abundantly requites.

ANNE BRADSTREET

The Beach Colony

HE TIDE WAS OUT; the beach was deserted; lazily flopped the warm sea. The sun beat down, beat down hot and fiery on the fine sand, baking the grey and blue and black and white-veined pebbles. It sucked up the little drop of water that lay in the hollow of the curved shells; it bleached the pink convolvulus that threaded through and through the sand-hills. Nothing seemed to move but the small sand-hoppers. Pit-pit-pit! They were never still....

The green blinds were drawn in the bungalows of the summer colony. Over the verandas, prone on the paddock, flung over the fences, there were exhausted-looking bathing-dresses and rough striped towels. Each back window seemed to have a pair of sand-shoes on the sill and some lumps of rock or a bucket or a collection of paua shells. The bush quivered in a haze of heat; the sandy road was empty except for the Trouts' dog Snooker, who lay stretched in the very middle of it. His blue eye was turned up, his legs stuck out stiffly, and he gave an occasional desperate sounding puff, as much as to say he had decided to make an end of it and was only waiting for some kind cart to come along.

KATHERINE MANSFIELD

All in Froth

Hark, hearer, hear what I do; lend a thought now, make
    believe
We are leafwhelmed somewhere with the hood
Of some branchy bunchy bushybowered wood,
Southern dean or Lancashire clough or Devon cleave,
That leans along the loins of hills, where a candycoloured,
    where a gluegold-brown
Marbled river, boistrously beautiful, between
Roots and rocks is danced and dandled, all in froth and
    water-blowballs, down.
We are there, when we hear a shout
That the hanging honeysuck, the dogeared hazels in the cover
Makes dither, makes hover
And the riot of a rout
Of, it must be, boys from the town
Bathing: it is summer's sovereign good.
By there comes a listless stranger: beckoned by the noise
He drops towards the river: unseen
Sees the bevy of them, how the boys
With dare and with downdolphinry and bellbright bodies
    huddling out,
Are earthworld, airworld, waterworld thorough hurled, all
    by turn and turn about.

GERARD MANLEY HOPKINS

Swallow-Time

THE EAVE-SWALLOWS have come at last with the midsummer-time, and the hay and white clover and warm winds that breathe hotly, like one that has been running uphill. With the paler hawkweeds, whose edges are so delicately trimmed and cut and balanced, almost as if made by deft human fingers to human design, whose globes of down are like geometrical circles built up of facets, instead of by one revolution of the compasses. With foxglove, and dragon-fly, and yellowing wheat; with green cones of fir, and boom of distant thunder, and all things that say, 'It is summer.'.... White breasts should gleam in the azure height, appearing and disappearing as they climb or sink, and wheel and slide through those long boomerang-like flights that suddenly take them a hundred yards aside. They should crowd the sky together with the ruddy-throated chimney-swallows, and the great swifts; but though it is hay-time and the apples are set, yet eight eave-swallows is the largest number I have counted in one afternoon.... Now, the swallows are, of all others, the summer birds. Ever since of old time the Greeks went round from house to house in spring singing the swallow song, these birds have been looked upon as the friends of man, and almost as the very givers of the sunshine.

RICHARD JEFFERIES

The Cloud Dwellers

O N ANOTHER MORNING after night rain the blue sky is rippled and crimped with high, thin white clouds by several opposing breezes. Vast forces seem but now to have ceased their feud.... These are the hours that seem to entice and entrap the airy inhabitants of some land beyond the cloud mountains that rise farther than the farthest of downs. Legend has it that long ago strange children were caught upon the earth, and being asked how they had come there, they said that one day as they were herding their sheep in a far country they chanced on a cave; and within they heard music as of heavenly bells, which lured them on and on through the corridors of that cave until they reached our earth; and here their eyes, used only to a twilight between a sun that had set for ever and a night that had never fallen, were dazed by the August glow, and lying bemused they were caught before they could find the earthly entrance to their cave. Small wonder would this adventure be from a region no matter how blessed, when the earth is wearing the best white wild roses or when August is at its height.

EDWARD THOMAS

Sweet Dejection

When the last sunshine of expiring day
    In summer's twilight weeps itself away,
Who hath not felt the softness of the hour
    Sink on the heart, as dew along the flower?
With a pure feeling which absorbs and awes
    While Nature makes that melancholy pause,
Her breathing moment on the bridge where Time
    Of light and darkness forms an arch sublime,
Who hath not shared that calm so still and deep,
    The voiceless thought which would not speak but weep,
A holy concord – and a bright regret,
    A glorious sympathy with suns that set?
'Tis not harsh sorrow – but a tenderer woe,
    Nameless, but dear to gentle hearts below,
Felt without bitterness – but full and clear,
    A sweet dejection – a transparent tear,
Unmix'd with worldly grief or selfish stain,
    Shed without shame – and secret without pain.

LORD BYRON

Morning and Evening

ATURDAY MORNING was come, and all the summer world was bright and fresh, and brimming with life. There was a song in every heart; and if the heart was young the music issued at the lips. There was cheer in every face, and a spring in every step. The locust trees were in bloom, and the fragrance of the blossoms filled the air. Cardiff Hill, beyond the village and above it, was green with vegetation, and it lay just far enough away to seem a Delectable Land, dreamy, reposeful and inviting.

MARK TWAIN

IT WAS NOT a bright or splendid summer evening, though fair and soft: the hay-makers were at work all along the road; and the sky, though far from cloudless, was such as promised well for the future: its blue – where blue was visible – was mild and settled, and its cloud strata high and thin. The west, too, was warm: no watery gleam chilled it – it seemed as if there was a fire lit, an altar burning behind its screen of marbled vapour, and out of apertures shone a golden redness.

CHARLOTTE BRONTE

Sea-Side Stroll

And now they walk upon the sea-side sand,
   Counting the number and what kind they be,
Ships softly sinking in the sleepy sea;
   Now arm in arm, now parted, they behold
The glittering waters on the shingle rolled.
   The timid girls, half dreading their design,
Dip the small foot in the retarded brine,
   And search for crimson weeds, which spreading flow,
Or lie like pictures on the sand below
   With all those bright red pebbles that the sun
Through the small waves so softly shines upon,
   And those live lucid jellies which the eye
Delights to trace as they swim glittering by.
   Pearl-shells and rubied star-fish they admire,
And will arrange above the parlour fire.

GEORGE CRABBE

A Stifling Heat

THE WEATHER now begins to be very warm, and tho' the thermometer never rises to the same height as in the West Indies, yet the want of air makes it quite intolerable. The evenings however are very fine, and we go out in Mr Rutherfurd's phaeton thro' the adjoining woods, and tho' the lightning flashes round us in these airings, yet it is a lambent flame, that we know will not hurt us. It is only the red lightning which sets the trees on fire, which is not so frequent, and is always attended by loud explosions and heavy rains. But the lightning I speak of is a blue flame, resembling that of spirits on fire, and is so common that no body pays the least attention to it. But the other is more dreadful than any thing I ever saw at home; it sets whole woods on fire and shatters the largest trees from top to bottom, and is followed by a storm of wind and rain, that of itself is terrible. But this is a necessary evil, and makes that circulation, which alone can purify the putrid air that rises from bogs and swamps.

JANET SCHAW

Evening Musings

Oh! how I love, on a fair summer's eve,
　　When streams of light pour down the golden west,
　　And on the balmy zephyrs tranquil rest
The silver clouds, far – far away to leave
All meaner thoughts, and take a sweet reprieve.
　　From little cares; to find, with easy quest,
　　A fragrant wild, with Nature's beauty drest,
And there into delight my soul deceive.
There warm my breast with patriotic lore,
　　Musing on Milton's fate – on Sydney's bier –
　　　Till their stern forms before my mind arise:
Perhaps on wing of Poesy upsoar,
　　Full often dropping a delicious tear,
　　　When some melodious sorrow spells mine eyes.

JOHN KEATS

Leaves of the summer, lovely summer's pride,
　　Sweet is the shade below your silent tree,
　　Whether in waving copses, or in fields
　　　That let me see the open sky.

WILLIAM BARNES

A Hundred Seasons

N THE AFTERNOON of June 20th, once more Bettesworth was at work among the potatoes.... we spoke of his work; and first he admired the potatoes, and then he praised his beck. 'Nice tool,' he said. I took hold of it: 'Hand-made, of course?' 'Yes; belonged to my old gal's gran'mother. There's no tellin' how old he is.' He went on to explain that it was a 'polling beck,' pointing out peculiarities hardly to be described here. They interested me; yet not so much as other things about the tool, which it was good to handle. From the old beck a feeling came to me of summer as the country labourers feel it. This thing was probably a hundred years old. Through a hundred seasons men's faces had bent over it and felt the heat of the sun reflecting up from off the potatoes, as the tines of the beck brightened in the hot soil. And what sweat and sunburn, yet what delight in the crops, had gone to the polishing of the handle! A stout ash shaft, cut in some coppice years ago, and but rudely trimmed, it shone now with the wear of men's hands; and to balance it as I did, warm and moist from Bettesworth's grasp, was to get the thrill of a new meaning from the afternoon. For those who use such tools do not stop to admire the summer, but they co-operate with it.

GEORGE BOURNE

Remembered Pageant

N THE WINTER TIME the Rat slept a great deal, retiring early and rising late.... of course there were always animals dropping in for a chat, and consequently there was a good deal of story-telling and comparing notes on the past summer and all its doings. Such a rich chapter it had been, when one came to look back on it all! With illustrations so numerous and so very highly coloured! The pageant of the river bank had marched steadily along, unfolding itself in scene-pictures that succeeded each other in stately procession. Purple loose-strife arrived early, shaking luxuriant tangled locks along the edge of the mirror whence its own face laughed back at it. Willow-herb, tender and wistful, like a pink sunset cloud, was not slow to follow. Comfrey, the purple hand-in-hand with the white, crept forth to take its place in the line; and at last one morning the diffident and delaying dog-rose stepped delicately on the stage, and one knew, as if string-music had announced it in stately chords that strayed into a gavotte, that June at last was here. One member of the company was still awaited; the shepherd-boy for the nymphs to woo, the knight for whom the ladies waited at the window, the prince that was to kiss the sleeping summer back to life and love.

KENNETH GRAHAME

Sources and Acknowledgments

For permission to reproduce illustrations, the publishers thank the following: Bridgeman Art Library, Barbara Edwards, Sam Elder, Mary Evans Picture Library, E. T. Archive and Michael Whittlesea.

The extract from *The Journals of Dorothy Wordsworth* is reprinted by permission of Oxford University Press.